NEW YORK

A PICTURE BOOK TO REMEMBER HER BY

Designed by
DAVID GIBBON

Produced by
TED SMART

CHATHAM RIVER PRESS

INTRODUCTION

In founding their own colony of New Amsterdam, on the site of the present city of New York, in the early 17th century, the Dutch also selected the best natural harbour on America's Atlantic coast. New York Bay itself had been discovered by an Italian, Giovanni da Verrazano, a hundred years before and explored by Henry Hudson, an English navigator who had been commissioned by the Dutch East India Company to find a shorter trade route to the Orient. When Hudson reached New York Bay he sailed up the river which now bears his name. From an ice-free harbour the Hudson River Valley provided an easy way through the Appalachian Mountains, and when joined by the Mohawk River became vitally important as a link between the farms and factories of the Middle West, the Great Lakes and New York City. This route contributed greatly to the development, from 1664, of New York, when New Amsterdam fell to the English without a fight and was renamed.

In 1690 the population of New York was 4,000. Fifty years later it was 11,000 and by the end of the 18th century approximately 28,000 people lived in this handsome and flourishing city. Its success was largely due to its ever-expanding trade with Europe and with the American interior, and its magnificent harbour was always crowded with ships, loading and unloading. Today, the port handles an enormous amount of traffic. The Hudson River is deep enough for giant passenger liners and cargo ships to reach the very heart of the city, berthing on the Manhattan Bank. At the East River piers other cargo boats unload tropical foods from South America and load manufactured goods from the numerous New York factories and warehouses. Newark Bay, which has developed rapidly since World War II, handles heavy, bulky articles such as coal and timber, and Bayonne specialises in the unloading and refining of oil.

Of the millions of immigrants who were attracted to the U.S.A., many decided to stay and make their homes in New York. Their different languages and customs, which they have to a large extent retained, resulted in New York becoming one of the most cosmopolitan cities in the world. Within its boundaries are distinct districts where large numbers of people of the same nationality live. Of these, Chinatown is probably one of the best known. Here, little English is spoken and street signs with their Chinese characters belie the fact that this is an American city. Pseudo pagodas are everywhere – even disguising the telephone booths – and there are shops and stalls selling exotic vegetables, fish and spices as well as exquisite objects of jade and ivory. The New Year is heralded by colourful parades in which symbolic and elaborate lions and dragons weave in and out of the streets and the air is vibrant with the sound of firecrackers.

Not far from Chinatown is Broadway, the home of the musical with its dazzling concentration of theatres and cinemas to suit every taste. The buildings that make the most lasting impression on the visitor, however, are surely the New York skyscrapers; tall fingers of glass and steel, soaring upwards and creating canyons of the streets, parts of which remain in perpetual shadow. It is these skyscrapers that have influenced urban development throughout the world. At one time the Empire State building was the tallest in the world, but it has now been superseded – even in New York – by the elegant twin towers of the World Trade Centre.

The imaginative complex of the Rockefeller Centre is virtually a city within a city. Twenty-one buildings provide offices, restaurants, banks, theatres, schools, gardens and even, during the cooler months of the year, an ice rink.

Another impressive collection of buildings is the Lincoln Centre for the Performing Arts. Here, opera, ballet, concerts and plays may be enjoyed in the most pleasant surroundings.

New York is also the heart of the American art world, not only for exhibitions but also for important auctions. Of the many fine galleries and museums the Metropolitan, Guggenheim, Whitney and Modern Art Museums contain some of the most superb collections in the world.

Another fascinating museum is that of the American Indian, where large numbers of artefacts have been gathered, reflecting the colourful and resourceful lives of the numerous Red Indian tribes. Finely beaded clothes, fearsome weapons and even scalps may be seen among the many exhibits.

Sports lovers are well catered for in New York. For spectators, Madison Square Garden provides the spectacles of ice hockey, boxing and athletics, whilst the vast Shea and Yankee Stadiums stage basketball and football. For those who want the exercise Central Park has the attraction of 840 acres of outstanding beauty in the middle of the concrete jungle of Manhattan. Various activities such as running, rowing, cycling and kite flying can here be enjoyed by everyone.

Also on Manhattan is Wall Street, the site of the world-famous Stock Exchange, where millions of shares are traded daily. This short street follows the line of what was once the walled northern boundary of the original Dutch Colony and which became a financial centre shortly after the Revolutionary War.

Overlooking the East River is the headquarters of the United Nations, occupying a prime 18 acre site comprising a 39 storey secretariat, the administrative centre, the marble and limestone General Assembly and a large library.

In addition to Manhattan, the city of New York has four other boroughs: Brooklyn, Queens, Bronx and Richmond, reached by many bridges and tunnels. Of these, the new Verrazano Narrows Bridge, connecting Richmond, Staten Island, to Brooklyn, is the world's longest single span bridge.

With a view over all the boroughs is the massive and unforgettable Statue of Liberty, which rests on its own island. This is a symbol not just of New York but of the whole of the United States of America. Designed by Frederic Auguste Bartholdi, the statue was a gift from the people of France to the people of America, commemorating a long friendship between the two nations. When dedicating the statue in 1886, President Grover Cleveland said: "We will not forget that Liberty has here made her home, nor shall her chosen altar be neglected."

The Statue of Liberty has withstood New York's salty air, and the city itself, despite financial problems, continues to be a great metropolis – symbolic of a great country of freedom and opportunity.

Standing guardian at the gateway to New York City's harbour, the incredible Statue of Liberty *left*, created by Frederic Auguste Bartholdi, is a symbol of Franco-American friendship.

Unmistakable and unforgettable, the New York skyline *above left* thrusts upwards to the sky.

Stretching across the East River is the distinctive Queensboro Bridge *left and right* which was completed in 1909.

The dramatic Brooklyn Bridge seen as night falls *top right*, connects Manhattan to Brooklyn, whilst *above* the gaudy street market strikes an incongruous note against the Manhattan skyscrapers in the background.

Manhattan is an island crammed to bursting point with monolithic structures of concrete and steel; never more evident than in this aerial view of Manhattan south *overleaf*.

The streets of New York *above* teem with life; whilst in these less familiar views of Wall St. *left and below left* the pavement hydrant is essential to the busy firemen.

The majestic City Hall *above left* houses the offices of the Mayor and *right* set amidst the skyscrapers is the formidable Stock Exchange. *Below* can be seen the Federal Hall Museum with a busy pretzel seller in the foreground.

Chinatown in South Manhattan houses more than 6,000 Americans of Chinese descent in its unique village atmosphere. It is a constant attraction, offering the visitor oriental curios of every description, whilst its marvellous restaurants have seemingly endless menus at reasonable tariffs. The bustling crowds, so typical of New York, throng the sidewalks. *Left* can be seen the exotic telephone booths with their pagoda-like roofs.

Gaily painted signs decorate the streets and colourful ideogrammatic newsstands grace the pavements in the picturesque Chinatown area. The annual New Year Parade is a particularly exciting spectacle and includes the necessary papier-mâché dragon.

uglia Restaurant

At the beginning of the century vast numbers of Italians poured into New York and established themselves in the Mulberry Street area which has come to be known as Little Italy. Each year, in September, the festival of San Gennaro is celebrated to honour the patron saint of Naples.

The magnificent aerial view *overleaf* of the sprawling city seen from the Empire State Building.

Amid the clamour and confusion of the city lies Central Park, seen here in many moods and differing seasons. This lovely oasis was created by Calvert Vaux and Frederick Law Olmstead in the mid 19th century and they contoured the park to the natural topography of the area. With its ice-skating rink, open-air theatres and restaurants it is a haven to visitors and residents alike.

One of the most impressive ways of viewing Manhattan is by helicopter, as these outstanding aerial views show. Not only can many of the skyscrapers be seen at close quarters but the narrowness of the island becomes apparent and the tremendous amount of office and living space concentrated in such a small area is quite amazing.

One of Manhattan's oldest and most
famous landmarks, which was built
at the beginning of the century, is the
Plaza Hotel overlooking Central
Park *above and left.* Behind the
hotel towers one of the most
spectacular skyscrapers in New
York *right and below* whose façade is
composed of black glass.

Manhattan by night *overleaf,* as
seen from the R.C.A. building, its
twinkling lights stretching back to
meet the horizon and dominated by
the central Empire State Building, is
a truly breathtaking sight.

The fascinating street life of New York vibrates with people and traffic alike, on 5th Avenue *left*, Grand Army Plaza *right* and *below* on 57th St; *bottom* can be seen one of the many refreshment stalls, this time outside Battery Park. The two unfortunate incidents *centre right and bottom right* are typical in a city of this size and density.

Fifth Avenue, New York's most fashionable shopping centre *below* is lined with exclusive shops *above and left*.

St. Patrick's Cathedral, with magnificent soaring spires, was designed after the noted Cologne Cathedral and can be seen *right*, and *overleaf* from the dizzy heights of the R.C.A. building.

Amidst the concrete network of a thousand skyscrapers, all jostling for space on Manhattan's crowded island, the Empire State Building, once the world's tallest, still towers supreme. In the superb aerial views seen on these pages the beauty of the structure for so long symbolic of New York is still readily apparent.

Countless lights from a thousand windows glint like diamonds in the midnight bay. Shining like a beacon behind the coal black skyscrapers is the Empire State Building in this night view of Manhattan *overleaf* seen from Brooklyn.

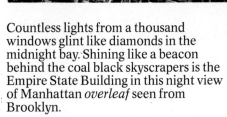

30 Rockefeller Plaza

The Rockefeller Centre occupies a three-block site whose central skyscraper is the R.C.A. building *above and right. Left* is the ice-rink which in summer is replaced by chairs and tables with gaily coloured umbrellas *pages 40 and 41.* Flags representing many nations flutter gently behind the Prometheus Fountain *below,* whilst the lovely Channel Gardens can be seen *left overleaf;* and *right* the magnificent bronze statue of Atlas on Fifth Avenue.

The distinctive yellow cabs of New York are seen on Fifth Avenue *above, right and top left. Far left* is the gigantic General Motors Building in the Grand Army Plaza and *left* the Public Library, considered one of the foremost in the world.

In the foreground *overleaf* stands the United Nations' permanent headquarters overlooking East River.

Radio City Music Hall is situated in the wide, tree-lined Avenue of Americas *above left, above, top and right*, where one of the main attractions is the "Rockettes", a group of thirty-six girls who dance the night away in high-kicking style, to the delight of many American males.

Madison Square Garden *left* is used for exhibitions, conventions and more notably for various sporting events. Towering behind it is Pennsylvania Station, terminal for Pennsylvania and Long Island Railroads.

Vast sheets of concrete, soaring skywards and allowing just a hint of blue to filter down to the pavement beneath, can often be oppressive for the visitor to New York, particularly during the summer months when the air hangs like syrup between the buildings.

The famous Flea Market on the Avenue of Americas *above and right*, with its colourful bric-à-brac, attracts many bargain hunters.

Car headlights blaze against the blackened monoliths lining Fifth Avenue *left*, whilst the Empire State Building rises majestically in the dark sky.

Broadway, the area around Times Square, is renowned throughout the world as the Mecca of Entertainment. Garish billboards and neon theatre signs light the streets by night adding to the glamour of this theatrical wonderland. By day *overleaf* the almos' deserted streets seem wan and forlorn after the night's frenzied activity.

Macy's Department Store *above left* starts at Herald Square and with its two million square feet of floor space is reputed to be the world's largest store.

Act I, the lovely restaurant *left*, at No. 1 Times Square is just one of the many to be found in New York.

Fountains play in the spacious Lincoln Centre where the graceful arches of the Metropolitan Opera House are floodlit by night *above*.
By day *right* this modern cultural centre is equally as gracious set against a cloudless blue sky.

Overleaf the signs, placards and garbage that are an integral part of New York life.

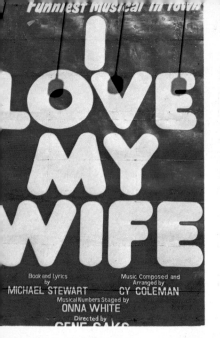

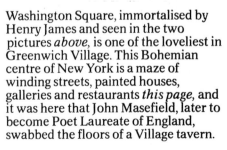

Washington Square, immortalised by Henry James and seen in the two pictures *above*, is one of the loveliest in Greenwich Village. This Bohemian centre of New York is a maze of winding streets, painted houses, galleries and restaurants *this page*, and it was here that John Masefield, later to become Poet Laureate of England, swabbed the floors of a Village tavern.

Still a fashionable quarter for aspiring artists, poets and writers Greenwich Village *this page* retains its quaint atmosphere in spite of becoming increasingly expensive. Once, however, and probably unknown to the many artists who now inhabit its environs, the village was the scene of public executions where New York hanged and buried its miscreants until 1828.

Park Avenue *overleaf* is New York's most fashionable and expensive thoroughfare.

First published in Great Britain by Colour Library Books Ltd
© Illustrations and text: Colour Library Books Ltd
Printed by Cayfosa and bound by Eurobinder - Barcelona (Spain)
This 1984 edition published by Chatham River Press,
a division of Arlington House, Inc.
Distributed by Crown Publishers, Inc., One Park Avenue,
New York, New York 10016
CHATHAM RIVER PRESS

Dep. Leg. B. 17.338/84